More Bagpipe Music

More Bagpipe Music: Poems on Scotland

Derek Alsop

First Published 2012
by University of Chester Press
Parkgate Road
Chester CH1 4BJ

Printed and bound in the UK by the
LIS Print Unit
University of Chester
Cover designed by the LIS Graphics Team
University of Chester

A catalogue record of this book is available
from the British Library

ISBN 978-1-908258-05-2

For Neil

CONTENTS

Preface   x

More than Shortbread   1

Castle Urquhart   3

Cuillin   4

St Kilda Revisited   5

Clan Macdonald on Skye   7

More Bagpipe Music   10

On Rannoch Moor   12

Scottish Mushrooms   14

The Painter of Animals   16

The Attraction of Mountains   18

Ladies' Day at Ayr   20

Waiting to Board   22

The Burials of Arran   24

Different Diets   26

Rear Window in Glasgow   28

Take Two Malts   29

Lower Largo   31

Dungeon Experience   33

Train Noise   34

Aberdeen Art Gallery   35

Moray's Houses Unvisited   38

The Biblical Garden, Elgin   40

Loch nan Eun   42

On Drawing Ben Gulabin   43

Thinking of Scotland   44

On Liathach   46

Stone   47

The Limitations of Cartography   49

Shieldaig   50

Scripture by Numbers   51

Seals at Portnahaven   53

The Birds of Jura   55

Songs for Scotland:
1. Mo Nighean Dubh   57
2. O Bone Jesu   58
3. Killiecrankie   59

Sights and Places Never Seen   60

PREFACE

None of these poems would have been written without my friend, Neil Margerison, to whom this volume is dedicated. Neil was born in Dundee, and though he left Scotland at the age of three, he went back to Blairgowrie every summer, as he puts it "to Gormack and his grandparents Will and Jessie McDonald, and a hillside covered in blackface sheep". Though my mother had fallen in love with Scotland over a number of holidays (she is a Bristolian, but calls the country her "spiritual home") I had never been, so, in 2003, I asked Neil to be my guide. We plotted our first trip together that year (I say 'we', but actually Neil, with his genius for planning, made this and all future arrangements). And so the first of seven tours began. One of our first hosts was Neil's own cousin, 'the mild and gentle farmer of Blairgowrie' referred to in 'Take Two Malts'. And it was on this trip from Edinburgh to Braemar, returning through Pitlochry, Dunkeld and Perth, that the first poem of what was to become this collection was written. The lorries of Perth woke me at five in the morning, and I found myself writing a poem that was finished by breakfast. It established a theme: tourist Scotland with its bagpipes, biscuits, woollens, tartan and monsters was not to be our Scotland, though we were certainly tourists. Our second visit was the most ambitious of the whole series, and proof of Neil's skill with an itinerary – flights to Edinburgh; a train to Inverness; a tour around Loch Ness, and then the train to Plockton. Neil again, on the best train journey of all our Scottish trips: 'The line from Inverness to Dingwall and Garve is coastal estuary and routine farming: notable more for the charm of the place names at Muir of Ord and (bypassed) Strathpeffer. But then along the lochs past Achanalt and Achnasheen into Glen Carron you ride between mountains on either side reaching up 700, 800 and 900 metres. The line runs on, through Strathcarron, along the edge of Loch Carron – in places, blasted out of the rock – to our stop at Plockton'. From there we crossed to Skye, and returned by the ferry to Mallaig. We stopped off at Rannoch, before the train to Glasgow, and home. In all – two planes, four trains, three taxis, a hired car, one ferry, and six hotels or inns in as many days. Future trips were never quite as ambitious, but it was always our aim to range across the country. In 2005 we went from Edinburgh to Lower Largo, St Andrews and the Spittal of Glenshee, staying at the lovely Dalmunzie House Hotel (with the best of welcomes from entirely Australian hosts). The following year we headed for Ayr, taking in the races before a trip to the beautiful island of Arran, and back via Wigtown (we both collect books). 2007 took us to Glasgow, Kinlochewe, Torridon and my favourite mountain Liathach, and Shieldaig. My love of malt whisky took us to Islay the following year (not only good drinking, but the kindest people we ever met), taking in Jura before returning to Glasgow. For our last trip, in 2009, we based ourselves in Aberdeen for a tour of Banff, Elgin, the Spey valley and Dunnottar. The reader of this volume will find the shape and shadow of these tours everywhere.

A word or two more about Neil is warranted, as his presence is everywhere in these poems. He is a consultant psychiatrist working in Hertfordshire, and the former husband of my wife, Linden. Though not as challenging as me, he has his eccentricities. He finds normal everyday decisions difficult (despite his logistical brilliance). If, as happened in Wigtown, a shopkeeper asks him if he would like a bag for his books, I make a hasty exit, as this is not an easy issue, and might result in complex negotiation. If a waiter asks him whether he would like the Scottish breakfast or the kippers, as at Kinloch Lodge, there might be some delay (resulting, on this occasion, in a Scottish breakfast with kippers on top). He also doesn't really do everyday conversation very well, but has the ability to draw out meaningful communication in ordinary circumstances. I remember one evening in Ardvasar, when, after ten minutes' chat with two American women, one began to share with him the suicide of her brother. While I was drinking glass after glass of Talisker and playing her friend at backgammon, he was helping this woman move on.

Neil thrives on vicarious enthusiasm. He enjoys nothing more than satisfying the obsessions of others. If I just mention, as I did in Inverness, the desire to draw, then Neil will disappear and return with a sketch pad, a set of pencils, some charcoal and a rubber. If I express an interest in the distillation of malts, then a trip to Islay and a tour of Caol Ila will follow. And he drove us everywhere (fifteen hundred miles on our fifth tour alone) with a bad back and ibuprofen (I don't drive, as it interferes with my drinking). As this volume of poetry emerged, Neil became its full participant, reading, correcting, appreciating, and occasionally begging to differ.

Of course, this volume, for all our touring, cannot 'take in' the whole of Scotland. Some of the gaps have been filled by imagination, some by the writing of others. 'Moray's Houses Unvisited' gestures towards the sense of incompletion, and the last poem expands on the same theme of 'Sights and Places Never Seen'. If I reflect on the experience of landscape, I would single out the formidable Cuillin (first seen from Plockton Hill), the monolithic Liathach, the desolation of the pass to Applecross, and the wildness of Rannoch Moor. Of cities, the ruins of St Andrews, the rough beauty of Glasgow, and the elegance of Aberdeen. Of islands, the circuit of Arran, the crossing from Skye and the hospitality of Islay.

The arts are important to the collection: the visual arts ('Aberdeen Art Gallery'); music (James Macmillan and Percy Grainger); and, of course, literature (though the title owes its origin to an Irishman, Louis MacNeice).

But the volume is not all celebration. Wherever you go in Scotland you find violent history: the bottle dungeon of St Andrews; the ruined walls of Castle Urquhart; the gruesome vault of Dunnottar; the massacre at Glencoe. Many of the poems reflect on Scottish history and its embattled allegiances.

A note on the dedicatees might be helpful. 'St Kilda Revisited' is dedicated to Sue Margerison, Neil's wife, who has the knack of digging out obscure and wonderful objects (including the postcard that inspired this poem). The rather cruel 'Clan Macdonald on Skye' is for Sheila, Neil's mother, herself a Macdonald, and an admirer of *Tristram Shandy*, alluded to in the poem (the satiric ill-feeling is not at all directed at her). 'More Bagpipe Music' is dedicated to Nigel Alexander, my mentor, and Head of Department when I arrived to study English at Queen Mary College, London in 1978. He died soon after I was thinking of him on the ferry from Skye, and some of the more flattering lines were read at his funeral (though I loved him at his worst as well as his best). I don't know

'F. B.' but he deserves the dedication of 'The Burials of Arran' as his epitaph is quoted at the end of the poem. 'Thinking of Scotland' is dedicated to Derrick Williams, my closest schoolfriend, and one of the best thinkers I have ever known. Percy Grainger's sublime setting of 'Mo Nighean Dubh' (the text of which I have done little more than plagiarise) explains that dedication. 'O Bone Jesu' is a homage to James MacMillan's brilliant setting, itself inspired by Robert Carver. The acknowledgement of Robert Burns for 'Killiecrankie' speaks for itself, and Jean Redpath's singing introduced the song to me. The final poem is dedicated to my wife, who wrote me a villanelle for my fiftieth birthday, so deserved one in return. Linden, amongst her innumerable other virtues, is a fine critic. She has listened to these poems at every draft. Whenever she was reticent in her approval of a line or an expression I knew she was bound to be right, so she is responsible for more improvements than anyone.

Final thanks go to my colleagues for their support and encouragement, particularly the poets Ashley Chantler and Francesca Haig, who made many suggestions, all of which resulted in changes for the better.

Derek Alsop, June 2012

MORE THAN SHORTBREAD

They seem to think it's Paris –
The five-in-the-morning lorries of Perth.
They shake and rattle their flatbeds
So keen, I imagine them running
On, past worn out clubs and pubs
Straight to the running Tay
At the road's end.
I did notice a tangle of metal at the
Bank's lap, so perhaps
It's no mere fantasy.

Fantastic, though, the run of that water,
Upwards, back through the days heading south.
To Meikleour, where a buzzard
Crossed us in sensurround widescreen;
Through Dunkeld and Pitlochry;
Back to a land of myth and mist,
Past a gloss of silly biscuits, woollies,
Malts and vacuous kilted nonsense;
Past brochured gossip of a glimpse of 'The Monarch'.

To the quick itself, as a herd
With no highway code takes
Space with it across the road
Up to the mountains, where,
Wheezing, we stumble after,
But stop, and edge right,
As two, then three, five stags
Gaze at our absurd intermission

With eyes of another time, but
Of this place the exact measure.

CASTLE URQUHART

The *Jacobite Spirit* out of Inverness
Throws back its spray of peat past
Castle Urquhart.
         Holiday-makers strain
To catch anecdotes of sack and ransack.
Some recent heritage joker sketched
A cartoon Nessie on the Urquhart plan,
Like 'Here be Monsters' on the seas of ancient maps.

That such a place should need implausibles!
We wake to sunlight, cloud and shadow;
The still loch, deeper than the thought of depth
Of tons of water-weight and counting.

'Sail the Loch. Live the Legend':
The launch proclaims its day-out pleasure trail.
Not here the slaughtering of Highland glens,
Nor here the murderous cold of mountain wars,
Or shame of lost, and lost again campaigns.
A comic plesiosaur's a safer theme.

The final garrison of this place
Held stronghold not for James, but for the other House,
Before the last petards began the end
That now speaks elegant ruin.

Tourists pass beneath their languages.
Farewell. Auf Wiedersehen. Vaarwel,
With its hint of orange.

CUILLIN

For four days now, peak and precipice,
Has loomed and lasted the Cuillin of Skye.
From train to Kyle, to Plockton Hill;
From banks of loch to Armadale;
From Armadale by ferry to Mallaig.
By tracks and boats, from shores and lesser slopes,
The Cuillin seems hospitable.

Not for those who climb:
A history of infamous ravines;
Of legends lined with loss, of
Footfall-edged calamity.

Sgurr nan Gillean; Sgurr a' Ghreadaidh;
Sgurr na Banachdich; Am Basteir.
A litany of meanings darkly glimpsed.

One day I will try the black Cuillin ridge.
I dream of it. My nightmares take me there.

ST KILDA REVISITED

For Sue

I love 'St Kilda's Parliament', as read
By Douglas Dunn, whose softened gutturals
Speak of 'solan goose' and 'sloke' with gentle
Loving strangeness. The poem's photograph
Of gathered men suggests a gaze beyond
The frame, both self-contained and sure of things:
Lives lived in the integrity of place;
Nobility beyond the dangerous work
Of scaling cliffs for improbable eggs.

I have another Wilson photograph:
Not here the Parliament with staring men,
But women and their children in a group.
They look like rock, built like stone cottages.
A gesture of a decorated hood
Does not disguise the cold. The women, used
To cold, hold for the exposure,
Arms crossed close, and hands in sleeves, frozen for
Their shilling or whatever Wilson gave.
With shock one notices their naked toes.
Explained as 'typical' – the footless hose.
Two weighty bundles sit there perched on walls,
I guess not remnants of the dispossessed,
But women's work, less glamorous than laws
And precipice and tales of derring-do.
If he said "cheese" he spoke a foreign tongue:
They squint or frown, but hold themselves in pose.

Beyond the grave they speak resolve, endure
Another day of bitter to the bone.

They will move off and wash the men's best clothes,
In freezing streams.

                    The men will then appear
In stories of democracy and law,
Embodying the primitive austere.

CLAN MACDONALD ON SKYE

For Sheila

Macdonald was his mother's maiden name.

He introduced me as the lover of his wife.
She welcomed me concisely, with her kitchen knife
Finely chopping carrots. There was no sense of shame.

She saw my reading list with Laurence Sterne.

She would have liked to study literature, not teach.
Her eyes were smiling at the thought of Tristram's
        breech;
And Phutatorius with his nasty chestnut burn.

Six years passed and I wrote a Ph.D.

On Burton, Rabelais, Cervantes, and Montaigne –
Their influence on Sterne, and his amused disdain
For learned men and their assured philosophy.

Two decades passed and I went to Braemar.

I bought a tourist gift, a silly Tartan tie,
Macdonald plaid – to please her son, despite the lie
Of Scottish heritage. Then in the hotel bar

We watched United win the league on Sky.

Next year we paid three hundred quid for just one
    night
To stay as guests of Clan Macdonald near the site
Of golden eagles nesting on the hills close by.

We thought we had to take a decent suit.

I bought a special case to carry mine about,
Through half of Scotland, always with resentful
    doubt:
I thought I'd make a sorry Highland clan recruit.

We took some drinks before the meal was served.

The people all around were wearing their best dress.
The suit, therefore, *did* come in handy, I confess.
The son-in-law, and even laird, put in a word.

The comments that they made were vacuous.

My friend was pleased with all the pomp and
    circumstance.
He rose to shake their hand. I joined the sycophance
And stood as well, my principles ridiculous.

We ate a meal served by the famous cook.

The lamb was clearly overdone, the soup too thick
To clean the palate, and the courses far too quick
To warrant special mention in the visit book.

My socialism met its nemesis.

I yearned for hostelries without the gloss of class
And bar-room meals and common wines served by
     the glass;
Communal toilets where you talk and have a piss.

We paid the cash and got a taxi out.

The shrill Macdonald woman welcomed in the day.
She shrieked "how glorious" as the taxi moved away.
And I imagined Campbells ready for a rout.

In retrospect Sterne would have liked Kinloch.

The kippers would have slipped into a waiting crotch;
Civility have lost itself in too much Scotch;
The laird would have forgot to wind the hotel clock.

MORE BAGPIPE MUSIC

For Nigel

"It's no go the merrygoround, it's no go the
    rickshaw",
he would proclaim with bitter drunken breath;
I knew that whatever it was he was saying was right.
"All we want is a packet of fags" and never mind the
    ferry pulling out of Armadale, sun
shining on the crossing view of Eigg and Rum,
where I remember Nigel Alexander,
who, like his father, did Shakespeare.

He gave crap lectures: a whole hour on *Macbeth*
passed with anecdotes of razor-blades hidden
in Glaswegian spuds. He could hardly pass the time
    of day:
his intense, venomous, fist-clenched anger
at the way things were would spit from him, even if
    you
just said "How are things?" The others – writers of
    merit –
were lost for words at his scandal. Political
    correctness
was waiting in the wings, and he was drinking heavy
against its hour. His speech was prophecy for us;
he gave us more than the rest with all their academic
    truths.
"So have I heard, and do in part believe" was his
    refrain.

Conspiracy and cloak-and-dagger stuff were all
        around.
Poison, Play and Duel – his book on *Hamlet* –
haunted by his father's presumably poisonous ghost.
His setting of *Othello,* brutal; his not-so-sharp-as-he-
        would-like
stage blades were directed at the throats of young
        innocents.
It was always sex with Nigel. He knew the driving
        force.
Suffice to say, some of us loved him.
He gave us the urgency of art, which I have never
        lost.

I think of him now, the Cuillin sharpening his void
as we pass beyond the mountains of Skye.

ON RANNOCH MOOR

Preposterous September sun placates
This wilderness. Nevertheless, the route
Bewilders still. Slowly, you step and hope.
Good ground still tests your ankles, knees and shins,
As grasses verge on the edge of nothing.
Heathers bristle your legs in the firmer
Betweens. Between, everything gives way, first
Foot plunging you in, peat-bog to the groin,
Creating sudden slapstick (comedy
An accident of climate – mist, storm or
Deluge just wouldn't see the funny side).
Loch and river bank give momentary
Respite, till we are pushed upland again
Into moss, morass and sodden moor.
Hour after hour the crazy patterns go;
Movement reduced to prepositions and
Deixis: up, down, in, out, on, here, there,
To and fro and under. The place treats us
Like its inadequate creatures, lacking
The legs for it, the balance, and the nous.
A hawk's-eye view must find our path deranged.
Directions without landmarks; general
Sense of 'over there'; Ordnance Survey
Scandal – satellite precision reduced
To arbitrary dots of stone; icons
Of heath and marshland; no rhyme or reason.
"Very wet, here, so put three 'marshes' down.
Firmer here – four stones. Scrub, here, more or less.
A bit of shore worth mentioning, perhaps."

A sense of giving up completely missed
This idyll of sand between two lochs, where
Now we rest, better than cartography.
But this land changes constantly; the chart
Might be right next year.
                          Later, from the train,
Southbound, it all looks picturesque, but now
We know it intimately and smile in
Complicity, dark friends of Rannoch Moor.

SCOTTISH MUSHROOMS

('This kind of thing is the stock-in-trade of a certain kind of
literary mind, but it provokes *me* to literal-mindedness.'
Richard Dawkins, *Climbing Mount Improbable*)

Poetic mushrooms often stand for something else.
For Sylvia Plath they're the 'bland-mannered' meek,
nudging their way to inherit the earth.
For Derek Mahon, the dispossessed oppressed
who moan for 'deliverance' from forgotten sheds.
Encroaching quietly or silently entombed –
they people metaphoric space.

I take them literally. Tautology
of mushrooms: emetic *russula*,
'the sickener', causes sickness;
the 'death cap' causes death.

A signpost points westwards towards Glencoe –
more miles than we have. We stroll instead.
A weasel takes its calculated chance
and dashes past; we stare into its voided space
finding, rather, a world of mushrooms.

We see a hundred species;
to each its proper parasitic hold.

Microcosm of hyphae and mycelium.
Mycologists' own metaphors:
crust and shelf and bracket fruits;
spheres, discs and saucers;

erect umbrellas; red-tipped glans;
picture-perfect fly agaric;
ludicrous puffball growths;
brains, and ears and fingers of fungus.
A forest of coral reds and oranges,
muddy browns and oyster greys.

The ordinary thought –
which can we eat? – is plainly silly;
taxonomy flounders, ironised, again, by names.
The 'false death cap' confirms death's lottery –
amanita citrina with its glint of lemon,
is edible, but to its unfamiliars
exactly like its truer alter other.

A path away from massacre,
these mushrooms might offer
good opportunity for symbols:
the chemistry of life and death, but

the highland dispossessed are dead and gone;
the meek would not set foot on Rannoch Moor.

Magic mushrooms (there must be
psilocybins here) might bring other visions.

But I'm happy with organic history;
the literal living spread of growing
things out of rotten dying things growing.

THE PAINTER OF ANIMALS

We met an artist, over dinner, full
Of passion, satire and intensity,
And venison and wine. The moor beyond
Did not impress. He had ideas in mind
Of other beauty found on distant isles.
I argued for the moor, without success.

"People just don't look," he said. "All they want's
A fag, a photo, and a souvenir.
I spend the whole day looking at a hare."

He mocked with us the Drumnadrochit way:
Its monster souvenirs; its tartan myths.
He gave advice about the malts; one of
The older Macallans, he thought, was best.

About him was a density of space.
We pictured wide impressive landscapes; burnt
Sienna sunsets; disdainful eagles
High above abandoned mountain views.

When we got home we thought to look him up.
His website gave us samples of his work.

Before us, prim and painful, were designs
Of garish sheep and butterflies, a kind
Of Woolworth's super-detailed photo-real.
For those whose art must look like what it is.

His smoking tourists might like these, I thought.

Meanwhile, the moor had darkened, wintered on.

THE ATTRACTION OF MOUNTAINS

The Reverend Nevil Maskelyne, Astronomer Royal,
Would doubtless have preferred to be somewhere else,

As he stilled, with numb hand, the plumb line,
Watching it lean to the density of mountain,
Drawn, obedient, to Newtonian law.

Not as exotic as his past adventure –
Observing the transit of Venus
From South Atlantic isles.

Four months out on Schiehallion
In eighteenth-century tents and bothies
Should lessen, you would think,
The attraction of mountains.

But still this lonely mountain slowly measured,
Against the altitude of autumn stars,
By its own mass, the mass of earth and planets,
Lending its old weight to the new science.

And was measured too, its heights drawn
Together in pencil, creating new contour-line
Cartography.
                    I look, two centuries later,
At the orange whorls of 'Explorer 386,
Pitlochry and Loch Tummel, West Sheet'.
And get the dawning of this age of certainty.

Apparently, when the work was done,
The universe duly weighed,
They had a party, with a fiddler.
The celebration got out of hand,
The violin was wrecked; the bothy burned.

So, cold empiricism ended in a piss-up.
I see these founders glowing in the fire,
Tuning, with outrageous jokes,
The music of the spheres.

LADIES' DAY AT AYR

The women, having their own Ascot; showing
off with ease, in high-street frocks, and sensible hats;
comfortable in manageable heels;
not crippled, nor teetering on the grass.
Like readers' wives, not glamour girls.

Always the ungainly food; the onions
you lean from as they slip aside
from impractical hot dogs;
bendy pints in plastic cups.

The horses, muscled to go,
twitchy, shining, tightened
into Sunday-best hairdos.

And other race days:

Sonia at Sandown,
red-nosed with cold (being from Tuscany);

Jim, intent, at Kempton,
calling me a "cute whore"
for a last-race coup;

the Gentlemen's at Windsor,
oak-panelled, with a gentleman
with brushes and lotions;

Chester, where girls in nothings,
precarious with drink, lock arms;
their suits, ahead, laughing off losses.

Now Ayr, too, settles into memory
under another September Scottish sun.

WAITING TO BOARD

There are some awful towns in Scotland.
Waiting for the ferry, in the naughty queue
for those who haven't booked,
counting the cars ahead of us, we could be stranded
at Saltcoats and Ardrossan, places so bleakly concrete
that a starling, glimpsed suddenly on a wall,
seems exotic, its iridescence starkly out of place.

We could go back to the local market
where tuneless cripples busk,
where charity shops need charity,
and stalls specialise in the unwanted:
arbitrary bags of biscuits; pounds of dubious meat;
toys of no franchise; clip-framed pictures
of twee children and preposterous pets;
hair ornaments for desperate girls;
cans of drink with acid, unknown, labels.

Strange that just south is an aristocracy of
golf, where glamorous Americans with names
like Weiskopf and Calcavecchia won the 'claret jug'.

Even the view – out across a swollen sea –
offers only a desolate tanker heading
deadly, inexorably, north.

No burgundy for us. We sip, suspiciously,
bad tea from cardboard cups.

Stranger still that, winning the loading bay,
we stand at the prow and lean towards
the beautiful bays of Arran.

THE BURIALS OF ARRAN

For F. B. 1831–1903; Arran 1860–1902

In and out of Arran, silly township signs
announce a flimsy heritage. 'Haste ye back'
says one, and in a bleak concreted place: 'Whit's your
     hurray?'

A man away from Arran on the ferry,
tells of his love for Somerset and Wells;
Goat Fell and miles of rain and swell are not for him.

Arran itself seems still in its own way:
not spoilt; not unspoilt; just as it happens to be.
No grand religious architect was here.

Astonishing in its lack of jumpers. As if
they might not have heard of Aran on Arran.
It doesn't mind our visit, but doesn't court us.

A drenching day, we tour the outer line of road –
spot sea-birds in our sea-bird-spotting book,
our umbrellas odd as Magritte's.

And everywhere the burials. Stones and cairns;
rings of liths around the cists.
(The etymology teases us – not

'cystis' for a hole, a cavity for death,
but Welsh, like Latin 'cista', for a chest:
a holding place and not an emptiness.)

24

These circles don't take your breath away
like the carvings of Wells, but the touch
of ancient stones is treasured, gradually.

At the northern tip of the island,
terns and curlews, oyster-catchers,
gulls about their business, like any other day,

against a driving weight of sky and sea,
a niche protects an absent tomb:
F.B. who died a year away from Arran,

which he loved more than any easier
southern shire, as those who loved him knew.
And here the 'aye' is homespun, honest:

'Aye rest is ours, and hereafter
in dreams, whether waking
or sleeping, will come
the visions of mountains,
of shore, and of streams
in our summer island home.'

DIFFERENT DIETS

(*The Times,* Friday, December 17, 2004)

Some witty editor drags two headlines
Together on the 'finally' page.

'Scientists prove death on Mars – in Scotland':
Research confirms Glaswegian Mars bars,
Batter-fried, ubiquitous.

We thought they were apocryphal, apparently;
An urban myth for those who think the Scots
Uncivilised.

But hundreds have them; painted up on boards
With sausages and saveloys and pies;
With 'fish from' prices.

They started as a bet, it seems,
In a chip-shop called 'The Haven',
That has since closed.

One owner says he sells, some weeks, three tonnes.

Elsewhere: 'Perfect meal postpones last supper':
Take fresh organic garlic, almonds, fish
And fruit, and proper chocolate, and you will
Live until redemption proves redundant.

Why do the Scots so rush towards death –
Their livers unpreserved by alcohol
Their lungs incurable of smoke?
Moving south beyond Loch Lomond,
Towards the outskirt railway slums of any town,
You see the logic of an early end.

Perhaps the beauty, always only just
Beyond the lights, most mocks the emptiness
Of life reduced to sofas, *Sun* and *Sky*.

Redemption's out. Religion left the church
For terraces: one football match that *means* a shite
Repeated time and time again, like purgatory.

Wash down that deep-fried caramel
With Teachers, then an Embassy or two.
When the heart is slowly breaking, break it quick.

REAR WINDOW IN GLASGOW

Sitting on a bed
in a hotel bedroom nine floors up,
though not on Plockton Hill, or Cairnwell:
another view of Scotland.

Two figures close together at an edge of sight;
a stairwell light goes on. He turns, descends
with care (it's steep) into another life.
No solipsist: I keep his after-presence live,
though now he's mine alone and doesn't know it.
In Hitchcock voyeuresque, I scan
for nakedness and nightgowns.

It strikes me, looking out, that anything will do for
        curtains,
high up, where walkers can't look in.
Impromptu makeshift anythings hang from hooks.
Lovers, at some point, noted this room
where now I sit.

'What is life,' wrote James, 'without curtains?'
And he was right.

TAKE TWO MALTS

*Open a bottle of Laphroaig whisky and you're opening
the heart of our community.*
(Laphroaig publicity.)

So easy to enjoy yet, like Skye itself, so hard to leave.
(Talisker publicity.)

I understand the mild and gentle farmer of Blairgowrie
who resists the single malts with principled but calm
    disdain.
For him the *Famous Grouse* will do the business without the
    fuss
at less than half the price. Not for him the vehemence of
Nigel, who pronounced with partisan violence on
malts and blends and whisky versus whiskey with an 'e'.

But I do want the sense, the taste of place.

I'd never been to Islay, but its landscape should be mild,
a few big hills, perhaps. No harshness in the taste;
just stretches of moss and grass and soil.
Full of peat; so 'feel the earth' the blurb demands.
Not sure I *want* 'the heart of the community' opened:
the long raw scar my tourist legacy.
Ludicrous, the leaflet invites you to claim 'your plot of
    land':
barcoded member of the Friends of *Laphroaig*.
In time, all Islay will inch by inch be owned by boozers.

'Nose: Phenolic' sounds better than 'like disinfectant';
I bathe my wounds in the glass.

Talisker has a different edge, 'the tall shadows of the
        Cuillin',
according to the label, haunt its sweet burn, which
runs all across the mouth, with a sting in the tail.
Skye itself *is* hard to leave:
the ferry breaks and cannot reach Mallaig.

It's this for me, though. The Thalas Gair,
its rock taking me roughly down the slope
to sleep, perchance to dream.

I wake at four a.m.
The bottle is unhinging me.
My good health fails.

Slàinte mhath.

LOWER LARGO

As I shall not make a paradise of Scotland, so I assure
you I shall not make a wilderness of it.
(Daniel Defoe, *A Tour Through the Whole Island of Great Britain*.)

Exotic – hints of henchmen, hurricanes
And holing up with Bogart – it is not.

We arrive, without intended tribute,
On a Friday, accidental tourists
At the 'Birthplace of Robinson Crusoe':
The 'real' Crusoe, though his fictions accrete.
As Selkirk was Selcraig, so Crusoe, Kreutzner;
Even Defoe, Foe – etymologies
Of alterity in the well-travelled.

Not here, in this kitsch statue's stony niche,
The 'real' man, brought before the Kirk on charge
Of 'undecent carriage'. No wonder he
'Did not compear, having gone away to sea'.

To sea we turn, away from low-tide stench
Of long-unprofitable estuary.
Birds of every northern species, and storm
On the horizon. Beyond, imagination moves
From Firth of Forth to sea and channel
Out to the great oceans. All journeys start
From one point.

       We head inland instead
Towards a hundred miles of high landscape,

Not out across three quarters of the globe.

But we will change too, as all journeys change,
Though our names, in this case, are likely to
Stay put, and our adventures bring only
Ordinary mythologies of place.

DUNGEON EXPERIENCE

Gaols and dungeons are entertainment, now:
a good day out for all the family.
'A feast of history's horrible bits'.
You can 'sample torture and punishment'.
The Visitor Book notes a girlfriend who
enjoyed her boyfriend playfully whipping
her supervised rear.
                But paranormal
evening volunteers really listen out
for electronic voice phenomena,
watch magnet movements for signs of haunting.

George Wishart, a student, teacher, scholar,
hounded for heresy, is carefully,
slowly, lowered the twenty-four feet to
the thirteen-foot diameter bottle
floor of St Andrew's dungeon. Waits, prays, eats
thrown scraps, clasps his cape closer to his white
skin, is comforted by a violent
night assault on Sea Tower gaol. Listens
in the cruel dark for steps, which come at last.
Hoisted up, out, into better clothes; show-
trialled, condemned, then burnt on the headland.
The bishops praise the glory of the Lord.
Carrion birds brave the swell and the heat.

Meet the team for an interactive tour.

TRAIN NOISE

"Your next station is Helsby."
The man with the bike learns
Virgin is fierce about pre-booking bikes.
At Warrington he shuffles from end to end
anticipating the order of coaches.
At Haymarket, Edinburgh: "That must be a stadium"
says a woman, looking at an evident stadium.
"Next stop is Leushers," says the man.
"It's Leuchars, with a 'cuh'," says a boy of ten.
"Your next station is Arbroath."
A twelve-year-old lounges, with new breasts,
her slacks below her bum crease,
as I read of paedophiles in Ian McEwan.
Next to me someone studies
The Climax of the Covenant.
He keeps himself to himself.
Behind me, eloquent, on mobile phone:
"The man is a disgrace: he's reprehensible.
There must be ombudsman proceedings."

Lives as strange as the coast,
on journeys that no biker, tourist, local lad, young girl,
Presbyterian or jobsworth litigant will remember.

ABERDEEN ART GALLERY

De gustibus non est disputandum.

But I know I'm right
about art I like and art I don't,
in Aberdeen's Art Gallery.

I don't like Hirst and Bailey's
'Jesus is Condemned to Die',
its glamorous gothic best reserved for album covers
by slash metal bands who'd eat your liver,
thump your testicles, for love.

I do like 'Gallowgate Lard',
Currie's intimacy of ordinary horror.
Livid face out of black,
bruised and bloodied lips,
eyes no eyes.

I don't like 'Jungled' by Gilbert & George,
their ugly colours, their alibi of church stained-glass,
for images of boyish masturbation.
They make me hate contemporary art,
which I love.

I went to see Francis Bacon's first ever Pope, but don't like
     him.
He seems too docile. I prefer my popes screaming.

I love Julian Opie's 'Sara Walking'.
There she is walking forever across a screen,
no more than outline, blocks for feet,
but woman for all that,
with her hint of bra, quite sexy.

I don't like Stanley Spencer.
His resurrection daftness leaves me dead.
(And I have to say the straddled girls astride the graves,
knees and legs spread wide for the Lord,
leave me feeling strange.)

I had a lovely chat with an attendant.
She liked Turk's 'Habitat' and so did I.
Cast in bronze, the down-and-out's sleeping bag,
weighed a ton. At first she didn't, but it grew –
its craft and its commitment;
its tendency to public anger,
reminded her of Emin's bed;
so we talked about Gavin and Tracey.

Goldsworthy's 'Sandstone Sea Hole' recalled
Dunnottar Castle in reverse. There, unrelenting waves
took millennia to shape the granite rocks.
Here, photos made a scene evaporate in a tide.

Time and death were in the gallery.

Uncomfortable, Macaulay Culkin's faked obituary.
Where everything you hate about America became
        unusual.
The awful child, *Home Alone*, gone home,
Became an elegy for all we lose, however bad.

I don't care much about art history,
But do hate those whose "kid could do that",
or who complain about the cost of a pile of bricks.

I like the urgency of judgement,
of being on the edge of what you know,
but knowing that it counts.

MORAY'S HOUSES UNVISITED

'You must go to Duff House.'
We didn't; at a turn in the road, a whim,
We left behind El Greco, Reynolds, Gainsborough,
    Chippendale.

'Step back to a bygone age,
And visit Maggie's Hoosie.'
We went by in a glance.
Her 'But 'n' Ben', her kettle, pot and kist,
Might have shamed the Duff Earls of Fife,
But this is only speculation.

We neither did 'discover and enjoy' the Salmon Bothy at
    Portsoy,
Its natural refrigeration uninviting in a North Sea gale.

The carnyx of Banff Museum,
Unseen.
(Somehow the word was enough.)

'Come and have a go!'
At Forndyce Joiners' Workshop.
We went the other way.

Any of these had shaped us,
If slightly: a painting here;
A battle there;
The haves and have-nots of local history;
Something forged.

Now we are unchippendaled,
Hoosieless, unfrozen,
Carnyxed, unjoined.

THE BIBLICAL GARDEN, ELGIN

The Bible has many lists:
begettings; devils; prophecies.
Here, one hundred plants –
Chapter and Verse,
'Thistles and thorns (see Genesis)'.
There, gardens lose their charm:
'Cursed is the ground because of you'.
Narcissus for scent (Isaiah).
There: 'All men are like grass,
their glory is like the flowers of the field;
the grass withers and the flowers fall.'
Olives speak for themselves.
The basil, though, is potless.
Generic biblical beans (Samuel) allow
Any old pulse: dwarf, runner, broad.

Sculptures, at intervals, present
Christ painted white (chipped);
unrecognised disciples.
Brown paint peels from febrile forms:
the worst, like lepers – no thumbs or noses.
Not Eden, but gardening after the Fall.
Already cured (the only miracle)
Samson, eyeful in Gaza.

The whole a themed, doomed, entry
to some flower show, where no gold
will gild the lily.

God and his planters could do better,
in this secular evening space,
where Elgin Cathedral, ruined,
watches over a tranquil corner
of our irreligious times.

LOCH NAN EUN

The lochan was a happening, a slow
Disclose – from glimpse to revelation;
Two thousand feet above, but still below
Encircling mountain mist. Exhaustion,
Quiet, and the fact and feel of ending,
As we crouch against the shore and rain.
Precipitous hours of descending
Past startled flights of grouse. The deer remain
Unmoved, still features of the higher ground.
The day's worst weather has become our own:
Now we are things of water, footing found
In sinking peat and heather, sliding stone.
   A hint of fear, a reassuring hand,
   A fellowship of time and place, of land.

ON DRAWING BEN GULABIN

Everyone should draw the landscape.
Here, matters of taste and judgement,
the hierarchies of art, beside
the point. To know somewhere you need
time with it.

      Ignore odd voyeurs
who look for evidence of 'art',
for something looking like the thing it is.
God only knows what they make of
my pencil marks, though I sense,
over my shoulder, reverence
give way to perplexity.

We all, of course, can do *something*
with a bit of charcoal or a pen.
There's nothing like the sense of line;
the shade of cleft; the sweep of tree
wind-swept; the scribble of the scree;
the easing of the rock to grass;
the hints of sheep; the specks of deer;
the flecks of heather; glints of gorse.

Everyone should draw the landscape
for a sense of time passing,
for a sense of time passed.

THINKING OF SCOTLAND

For Derrick

It's clear I'll not climb Liathach.
It's true the Cuillin is for others' plans.
But if I think of Cat Bells
and other reasonable English slopes
(with comfortable Wainwright names)
it leaves me relatively cold.
Manageable, green, inviting fells,
like Auden's limestone moderation,
will not do.

       I want the wilderness,
the empty and the desolate,
the feel of ancient times uncivilised.
I don't want Kendal Mint Cake.
I want my mobile *not* to work.
I want to know I *cannot* bag
the mountains, like the sad collector
otherwise I am. I want beyond and other.

Once, at twelve, with Derrick Williams,
my friend, I meant to trek the landscape
and camp a tent somewhere in Somerset.
We planned the trip in secrecy, lest
nervous mothers hear the plot and smother it.
We larked about, equipment minimal, but prepped,
the beers exciting in the packs; – then bottled it,
walking, instead, five miles to Bath and back.

It was, I know, my fault. I shrank.
Intrepid failure often was my theme.

But themes outgrow the practice lost,
and still I lie curled in the bed,
thinking of Scotland: its cold mountains
ever, never, to be tried.

ON LIATHACH

The path is kind, considerate, as if
Against the weight of vertical grey cliff
Stiff starts are pointless gestures. Liathach
Won't show itself for half-an-hour, but back
Behind us other mountains, big enough,
Observe our meagre purpose: know the stuff
That dreams are made on will not do up here.

Suddenly the massive towers appear,
Clouds gathering around their height of stone,
Suggesting geographies of tales unknown.
No ordinary poet would invoke
This muse. I climb, a mock-heroic joke
Of man, on a neglected outcrop; yet
Begin to learn the mountain's alphabet.

STONE

'Sometime round about the 1580s the phrase *in the nick* or *in the very nick* began to be used for the critical moment, the exact instant at which something has to take place. The idea seems to have been that a nick was a narrow and precise marker, so that if something was in the nick it was precisely where it should be.'

I have a stone in my pocket.
I keep it about me, in the here and now,
This rock of ages:

Of the earliest of animal eras –
Proterozoic;

Composed of sand, settling, sitting down –
Arenaceous,
Sedimentary.

Five hundred and twenty million
To one billion years ago
It settled in Torridon.

When my ancestors were sponges.

Compact and dense and crystalline,
Ochre and grey and brown
Sand-paper stone,
Abrading, gripping, tense.

Lifted from the feet of Liathach,
From the old grey one,
On September the ninth, two thousand and nine,
Common Era,
When it settled in my coat,

Arrived in the wrong geology,
The trias of Cheshire,
South, by motorway.

Precisely where it had to be,
In the nick of time.

THE LIMITATIONS OF CARTOGRAPHY

'He makes the shadow he pursues' is right.
Excitement makes me nearly always wrong.
I think Glen Etive is Glen Coe; obscure
Grey masses are my Liathach until
The old grey one is manifestly there:
The right side of the road, not on the left.
Once, looking from the ferry I was sure
I saw the Cuillin; it was only Rum.
By car, I commentate on all I see,
With piles of maps around my arms and feet:
And to the left we see Loch Linnhe; or
Perhaps Loch Leven. No, surely Linnhe,
Or Loch Eil. And here we see three sisters;
Oh, no: they are the sisters of Kintail
(All five). Thank Christ I'm not a proper guide:
The muddled Chinese whispers of my route
Re-drawing, bit by bit, the Scottish map
Arsy-versy.   But I'm on holiday;
My cock-ups are leisurely and without
Consequence, and when I look up I leave
The maps in disarray and, open-mouthed,
Take in the glories of the glens and lochs
And mountains upon mountains unnamable.

SHIELDAIG

Pretty, but unpromising, is Shieldaig,
Above itself, a social-climbing set.
People on the world's edge, dressed for dinner,
Where local waitresses forget the script
Of highland something with a haggis jus.
So spick and span, the 'town' a minute long,
You feel you cannot fart; but walk towards
Temperance Brae, intemperate, after dark.
Earlier, the night was edged in red
And white. Now all is black, but for the stars,
And starlight on the loch, immaculate.
I find a perfect bench. The island, grey
And dim, ahead (donated, so it's said,
By some Americans, the Armisteads)
Has ospreys, nesting in the pines, not seen
But heard. They screech. Respect for heritage
Civility, propriety, is not
Their thing. Above me shine a thousand stars.
I only know Orion and The Plough:
But they and all the rest, unnamed, unknown
Put Shieldaig in its place: a street, a club,
A restaurant, some B&Bs, a pub.

SCRIPTURE BY NUMBERS

Before the tower, that uneasy space
Where selling stuff nudges devotion.
Embarrassed bookmarks, postcards and cassettes
Edged by Sunday School Jesuses:
One – sausage crucified, unsmiley face,
Fingers and toes like rotorblades;
Two – noughts and a cross of waving limbs
Impaled on long balloons.

On the prayer tree, a widower
Complains to his ethereal other half:
About twenty years alone.
Others, too, count down the anniversaries.
Death is essentially numerical.

On May the thirtieth, nineteen ninety-two
A peal of five thousand and twenty-two
Plain Bob Caters took three hours, twenty-seven.
The tenth Duke of Argyll built the dead-
Commemorating tower
Where Jonathan Paul Carpenter,
Leaving his entry,
'Rang as a boy'.

The ringing boy rang the second heaviest
Ring of Ten Bells in the world;
And probably knew his scripture.

For 'painful memories', a souvenir suggests,
Try 1 Corinthians 15:9.

Corinthians are 'bittersweet' in verse 6:10,
Galatians 'watch their step' in 5:16.

Watch our steps we do:
One hundred and seventy six.

Tickets cannot be exchanged.
For what, we wonder?
Children must be accompanied
By ticket-holding adults
(Fee-dodgers, presumably, not trusted).
Any old dog, dogmatically, is banned.
The incorrectly 'handicapped' are just warned off;
Strictly, you cannot eat or drink or smoke.
There is no liability except in case of death.

Now we must make our way
Down the twisting numbers,
Shortly after the closing bell
At 4:58, two minutes before
The end of time.

SEALS AT PORTNAHAVEN

Crouched in the wind at this western limit,
Staring out, between the last two islets of Islay:
The Atlantic, landless until Newfoundland.

Binoculared, we tour the sky and seas.
We know a heron when we see one,
And, seeing one, approve.

Bobbing near rocks, though,
Is a seal, and, learning the geometry
Of seals, eventually
Even that cold, sleek, crescent rock,
Anvil of ocean gales,
Turns out, in fact, to be one.

Then dips down, comes up
Nearby, looking at our looking,
Asking after us, our why and wherefore.

You would forgive the island distance and detachment,
Far out from anything.

But we are accepted; an engineer
Describes the hawk he saw today,
Out fixing cables. A builder gives us
Tablet, made specially by his wife.

Meanwhile the seals slip, unfussed,
Into seas to freeze imagination.

They make no bones about it,
And are prepared to pass the time of day with
Anyone who happens on the edge of things.

THE BIRDS OF JURA

Dizzy lexicography of birds –
Its unkind ravens and exalting larks –
An expectation of ramblers.

I-spy perfection would collect,
From each habitat, the choice.
How, though, to judge?

By shore, a curved familiarity of curlews;
Self-evidence of oystercatchers;
Out of any zoo, a routine of herons;
Leaves only rock pipits,
Unknown, unrecognisable.

By bay, of any park, mundanity of mallards;
Various gulls, black-backed, headed (or not), still gulls;
Obviously different cormorants, obviously posing;
Leave only the red breasted merganser
Unknowable, unseen.

In fields, the hooded crow, (hood or no) but a crow;
We could not not know a pheasant, having plucked and
       eaten him.
The starling, too, breasts instant recognition.
Another pipit (meadow), or stonechat –
None the wiser neither – are all that's left.

By farm, by God, I know a robin or a blackbird
Can even tell my tits (great; blue; coal),
But I don't know dunnocks or reed buntings
(By woods, apparently, the latter).

I learn my lesson:
I know already only what I know.

The wages of handbooks and binoculars?
That I will die not knowing, I know,
A hawk from a handsaw.

SONGS FOR SCOTLAND

1. MO NIGHEAN DUBH

For Percy Grainger

The poet and his dark-haired lover,
Despite the blasts of winter weather,
Are still together:
Other shores to share, though never
This one view to see.

Gone is that glen, the heather;
Past, the momentary pause of whether
She would take him now, forever,
'Fu' o' mirth and glee'.

The hills were bright,
And on that last and lovely night,
Together on Knockgowan's height,
An elegy of time and sight,
The future yet to be.

SONGS FOR SCOTLAND

2. O BONE JESU

For Robert Carver and James MacMillan

O bone Jesu,
Through centuries of faith and fail,
O piissime Jesu.
Glissando, portamento
Voices slide and slither,
Shaped by serpents.
O dulcissime Jesu.
As if mere incantation of His name will heal,
From Carver to MacMillan,
From Flodden to the falling towers of our times.
Music of the gods, or God, or man,
Alone or in communion.

SONGS FOR SCOTLAND

3. KILLIECRANKIE

For Robert Burns and Jean Redpath

On hearing 'Killiecrankie', Katie 641, online:
'We may be defeated, but we still stand proud'.
The Scots, that is. But if she had been
where he had been, she wad na been sae cantie O.
No certainty anywhere but blood.
Claverhouse, to different Scots
'Bluidy Clavers'; 'Bonnie Dundee'.
Brutal killer of the covenant or
martyr to the cause of James.
"How goes the day?" he said, at last, some say:
well … well for some, for others dire.
Another Scot leapt famously the Soldier's Leap;
he has his postcards too, perhaps a song,
though of King William's clan.
One fell, another jumped, both leant
a mess of history; legacy of doubt.

SIGHTS AND PLACES NEVER SEEN

For Linden

For sights and places never seen
I offer up this final list,
Acknowledging what might have been.

The marriages of Gretna Green;
The Isle of Rum, its ancient cist.
For sights and places never seen.

For most things north of Aberdeen.
The ospreys, golden eagles, missed;
Acknowledging what might have been

If my binoculars were clean.
Harris, Lewis, North, South Uist –
For sights and places never seen

Include the islands in between.
The monsters that may not exist –
Acknowledging what might have been.

For every mountain and ravine
Unclimbed; for lochs lost in the mist.
For sights and places never seen,
Acknowledging what might have been.